SONGS OF A PSYCHIC SEAHORSE

(faithfully translated from modern seahorsian
a fluid subaquatic language best known for musical candor
& dynamic counterpoint)

STEPHEN ROXBOROUGH

NeoPoiesis Press, LLC

2775 Harbor Ave SW, Suite D, Seattle, WA 98126-2138
Inquiries: Info@NeoPoiesisPress.com
NeoPoiesisPress.com

Stephen Roxborough – Songs of a Psychic Seahorse
ISBN 979-8-9858336-5-2 (pbk)

1. Poetry. I. Roxborough, Stephen. II. Songs of a Psychic Seahorse

Library of Congress Control Number: 2024931721

First Edition

Cover Design: Dale Winslow and Stephen Roxborough
Cover Photograph: Stephen Roxborough

Printed in the United States of America.

FOR THE KIDS & PARENTS
OF OUR GREAT GLOBAL
DYSFUNCTIONAL FAMILY

CONTENTS

foreword:

all 46 exquisite varieties
of the pipefish family known as
seahorse
        belong to the genus
        hippocampus

ancient greek for horse (hippos)
& sea monster (kampos)

the hippocampus is also a small
multi-layered region of the human brain
in the shape of a seahorse
embedded deep in the folds
of temporal lobe
                        the hippocampus
        plays a major role in learning
memory and the regulation
of behaviors needed for survival:
feeding fighting & sex

hippocampus is also crucial
for long-term memory formation
& retrieval

the psychic seahorse sings new songs
of innocence & experience
depicting the practical & mystical overlap
of both
        how teacher becomes student
& the perpetual looping after-effects
of quantum entanglement

the nose knows

there's a direct expressway
from olfactory to hippocampus

where our deepest memories
are created in mood & drift

the only sense that never sleeps
smell even works in a coma

nose always pulls us back
to those indelible moments of

atmosphere & yesteryear
the attraction of waking up

to the maillard reaction
on a waft of spluttery bacon

the pure milky calming scent
of each newborn baby

or potent whiff of pheromones
from a distant blissful lover

when we become orphans

said the old seahorse to his fry
because our parents left the building

those two great libraries close down
the family tree splits into branches

that swim in different time zones
& often don't loan to each other

who carries all the memories
of our primal personal history?

who cares about the great uncle
that became a conscientious objector?

who knows about the witty cousin
noel coward wrote songs for?

who remembers the relative
that struck a lode of alaskan gold?

who knew the internal psyche
of the world's greatest oddsmaker?

who chooses what memory remains
& what gets rejected forever

as we all fade & eventually
evaporate into the next

in the beginning there was milk

wet warm & sweet fresh from
the source of human kindness
& the milk was good

until juice & fruit from trees
of the tropics introduced
a sweeter exotic temptation

yet when the grain of cane arrived
the brain went insane to the store
for the many flavors of more

then every day in the loudest way
the kids screamed for ice cream
& year-round halloween

seems even old men drinking
like teens can't wean themselves
still in search of human kindness

still boiling the brain to coddle
still sucking on something sweet
& fluid from a bottle

yet in the beginning it was fresh
from the source of human kindness
warm from the source of likeness

my generation started strong

scorned materialism
marched for civil rights
protested war
rallied for female equality
but in the end we turned out to be
another disappointment

war became a superbug
fast-talkers spread like oil slicks
news fused to propaganda

the giant anaconda of big pharma
swallowed us whole as corporate pirates
& spineless politicians
embezzled national treasure
then we sold out to hostile reptiles
for dollars & tiny pleasures

we got stranded in slander
scandal bankers & tangle

they brought us inside to hide
& divide us until we abandoned
our better angels
& collective casablancas

now i feel great communal shame
a deep disgrace & dishonor
for not fighting stronger
longer & harder

we didn't even pick up
after ourselves

the first time my son planted

a deep gash in his unblemished knee
& vivid burgundy gushed
down his leg
                    he ran to me in tears
because he thought he'd lose
all his blood & die

when i said let's go to hospital
          to get a few stitches
he ran away so fast
it took me three minutes
to catch & carry him to my car

i strapped him in his car seat
all the while he cried
          i'm still bleeding!
          i don't want to die!

later that night
long after the kids went to bed
& the trauma of the drama
          stitched & calm
i reflected upon
how i died a little that day

but it was a good death

over a glass of red wine i realized
we shared the same blood
& his pain became mine

the kids today are smarter

they got more at their fingertips
than any ten generations
                         put together
& yet all they want to do
is devour pizza
play games & dodge chores

what'll happen to the kids
who don't play outside anymore
who don't pick fruit
climb trees or swim lakes
who don't play capture the flag
kick the can
          skip rope
                    red rover
                              hopscotch
or watch sunsets & night skies
who don't ride ocean waves
wish on shooting stars
relax in the grass while they discover
animal shapes human faces
& cosmic signs in clouds?

the self-appointed shut-ins
the digital dandies
                    & lost inside boys

imaginations warped & captured
by pixel pixie worlds

kids think grown-ups have all the fun

they drive the cool cars & deluxe trucks
& always decide where to go

they eat all the ice cream they crave
& they're allowed to be cranky & angry
snobby & snooty & stubborn & lazy

they don't do stupid chores
        or hours of boring homework
they don't have to share the TV
the new computer or prize controller
& they're never forced to eat liver
to be rewarded with sugar

they can demand peace & quiet
& get money from machines

they stay up as late as they want
go to parties whenever they like
& don't need permission to see friends
play outside or eat the last cookie

they save all the best movies & games
& toys & drinks & drugs & fun
for themselves

best of all they don't have parents
bossing them around anymore

        to the kids it all looks easy
dream peach privileged
as if parenthood
is the ultimate superpower

adults think kids have all the fun

they get to race big wheels & spin
on a dime & laugh & crash & never worry
about collision insurance

they get all their food & clothes
& toys & soothing made & paid for

they're allowed to be cranky & angry
& snobby & snooty & stubborn & lazy
while parents try to inspire their best
with the least amount of stress

they get spoiled & pampered & coddled
& every few years their private room
gets remodeled

kids get sheltered from the storms
& thorns of tides & divides of relationships
        they're guarded from the weight
& grind & fear of deadline walking

they don't know the building pressures
triggered by bills & pills & grown-up ills

years ago we'd be beaten at home
& even school yet today it sounds absurd
for a kid to be seen & not heard

all vampires & zombies

they're killing the dead
singing blood-sucking blues
riding a tidal wave of animal
in a cycle of nonstop news

they got shiny silver bullets
& pointy gothic crosses
they got vials of lovers blood
hanging like albatrosses
they got bible black lipstick
& crackerjack skull tattoos
they got booby-trapped bunkers
& stockpiles of lifestyle tips
to outlast the eclipse
of the looming apocalypse

not a lame game anymore
when death knocks on your door
& they're killing the dead
singing blood-sucking blues

super viruses grow stronger
than the strongest kryptonite
while blood grows weaker
& the world's in a fever
seawater rises to a new crisis
as fresh water evaporates
extremes seem to dominate
& the straits get more dire
our entire planet dissolves
in perfect conflict hellfire

not fake news anymore
when death knocks on your door
& they're killing the dead
singing blood-sucking blues

the kids find this amusing
as if the joke's on someone else
as if the meek get the last laugh
as if the world they inherit
just carved its own epitaph
& all the stardust beauty
has suddenly become
a mediocre horror movie
twisted into a tribal spiral
video game for survival

we're all vampires & zombies
troops of subgroups to abuse
cause they're killing the dead
singing blood-sucking blues

not a blame game anymore
when death knocks on your door
& they're killing the dead
singing blood-sucking blues

ode to laundry

laundry is my meditation my anchor
my answer my foundation my center
my charge my urge my church

water soap clothes wash spin rinse
dry fold & back into the holy order
of deep dresser drawer
a beautiful ordinary primary chore
repeat once a week or more

load after load after motherload
a piece of me goes into each machine
around & around & i calm down
as everything moves in a perfect
swishing humming sound

select-o-matic anti-static turbomatic
temperature speed & agitation control
bless my soul bless my spotless soul

i pray to the gods of underwear
& all the hues & muse in jeans of blue
please let the load in this machine
come brighter whiter color clean
set my grass & bloodstains free
set my stress & migraines free

may this holy load be my guide
my vital mission & spirit ambition
my anchor my answer
my prayer for purification
my perfect earthly order

my wordless sermon to salvation
& my temporary liberation
to escape the manic insanity
& daily jumble of mud & clutter
in the wrestling-ring chaos
of raising sane offspring
for a doo-dad madcap world

somewhere in the garage

by the archives of lost & forlorn
resides an art bag of preschool paintings
            composed when the kids
were unselfconscious
& prolific
two or three masterpieces a day
for a couple of years

my miniature minimalist vincent van
jackson de koonings

        big bold brave joyous buoyant
reckless impatient contagious
audacious brushwork
                        sometimes zen
                        sometimes chaos
always full of spontaneous memory
& innocent energy

before self-criticism indecision
comparison judging grades & doubt
clouded creativity
                        always willingly
            effusively intuitively
the kids knew the beauty
of art for art's sake

doing nothing is harder

i watch the kids & marvel
how they're not afraid of failure

out on a limb
swinging for the fences
diving for the end zone
winding up a long slapshot
          not looking back
                    blazing new trails
jumping six steps of stairs
fantasizing without fear
testing & trying & striving
in a constant state of discovery
falling & rising
reaching & achieving
beyond themselves

they teach me how failure
is the new translation of inspiration
they give me the courage to fall
fold bomb flop & crash
then pick up
dust off
& always push on

style drives their bus

their ID their password their code
their club
their secret tongue
how they try to fit in by following
the in-crowd just enough
but not too much

square store high-rent stolen fashion
front window exposure
corrupts the craze
          dilutes the dialect
ends the trend

way back when i was one
of the kids in anti-system attire
floral prints with billowy
cuff-lace sleeves
old seahorse thrift store vests
striped bell-bottoms
water buffalo sandals
or bare feet
but today the fashion-worm
has turned to serious sport

500-dollar basketball shoes
that will never squeak on hardwood
take the fun out of the form
& change our language
to capitalism

make us believe we need
a regular suit & tie job
just to keep our feet in vogue

we're all creatures of habit

the kids are no exception
as i watch their pavlovian reflex

their email text google social buzz tingle
vibrate impulse ring-tone instinct
or the self-absorbed episode
for more tiktok snapchat
youcam upload

even hipsters joined at the hip
& long in the bluetooth approve

she tells you what to do
where to go & how to do anything
dozens of better intentions
even plausable answers
to Big questions

listens to all your problems
from condoms to toxins

she's your new best friend
but she's not forever
& the kids think
that's the best part of the plan

she's discreet & upbeat
knows when to advance or retreat
she won't ever break down
she just becomes obsolete

the game existence

the kids complain
we didn't ask to be born
                you decided to have us
         you wanted us & you made us
we don't even know
why we're here
no surprise we're confused
& no wonder we don't know
what's going on

            old seahorse nods his head
            as if he's heard it all before

he ponders their teenage logic
& says
how can you be so sure
of what you don't know?
                perhaps your return
         to earthschool
was your idea
& you chose us as parents
because you thought we were
your best option

i've heard when you reincarnate
your memory is wiped clean
so you don't carry
too much past around
so the game of life becomes
more spontaneous
less routine
& you fill your hippocampus
with new collections of questions
impressions progressions possessions
obsessions & lessons

        you just need to figure
        how to hack the current matrix
        & manifest a better reality

the kids complain
we're not interested in stories
not amused by your cafeteria religion
& your artless high school
matrix metaphor
we need facts you can prove
because life is really hard
& expensive & there's nothing
we enjoy about it

then i suppose old seahorse says
our indian buffet lunch date
is out of the question
        & the kids quickly respond
no no no
we didn't mean that

(out of the blue) my oldest announces

i want to be the grim reaper
every halloween

taken aback i ask why

because he's the most powerful
dude on earth

sooner or later
he takes everybody out
then adds for good measure
& emphasis
        even you dad

so i buy him a plastic scythe
a long black cape with faceless hood
smear fake blood on his blade
& wait

for the inevitable knock
on my door

we were all kids once

pre-middle age & caught up
in the whirl of lust & competition
still thinking we're going somewhere
crossing borders expanding matter
changing intergalactic order
but merely treading water
in the fountain of youthful soup
peering & engineering through
that blissful ripple mystic nipple
triple chocolate raspberry
mortal portal drizzle pixel
purple haze parfait

before we realized the universe
won't solve anything by devolving
into amplified ego ambitions
before the potent omen allure
of our insecure premature
neo-placebo conditions
merge with our perfect cookie jar
open-bar wannabe dream-star avatar
& hound us down the rabbit-hole
of ubiquitous insignificance

before we noticed everyone
chasing tails round & around the sun
until the hearts of parts fell apart
& our cosmic shoelaces came undone
before we saw through the bamboo
illusion of the broken time-screen
trying to get over there & dying to be
someone rich or maimed by fame

yet still as kids & believing still
in powers of great dreaming
& healing & feeling the freewheeling
thinking we can change the world
with one picture
one poem totem acorn song
or one mysterious moonlit kiss

the fashion of fads

flat tops & beatle wigs
beanie babies & hula hoops
low-rise & deep cuffs
pop rocks & pet rocks
mini-skirts & maxi dresses
panty hose & bobby sox
hot pants & culottes

platforms & earth shoes

smiley faces & face tattoos
streaking & skinny-dipping
handlebars & goatees
skinny ties & wide lapels
stovepipes & bell-bottoms
mutton chops & power beards
bullet bras & landing strips
jet-set getaways & acid trips

be-bop & hip-hop

goldfish swallowing
& jello wrestling
beer pong & dance marathons
the clapper & clackers & rappers
& flappers & slackers o my!
the kids make it up & the kids
take em down

sometimes a new generation
unconcerned with reverberation
embraces the echo in retro
& they return to haunt us
as if want to be wanted again

the kids have discovered

how to push my buttons
bust my balls & break my heart
all at the same time

they've studied me for years
as if i'm their maker & jailor

        the backlash & clash
of our stubborn blood
& defiant seahorse DNA
        standard hazards
& consequences of the job

the safest way of fighting back
undermining authority & flexing
teenage angst
        we reject & resist
    defy with anger
sometimes snap
& crack

then let go & heal

     brings us closer
helps us grow up together

the kids know everyone is watching

& they don't really care
we've got nothing to hide they say
but it doesn't matter anymore
cause privacy is now a luxury
no one can afford

phone records are forever
cameras follow your every move
the eye in the sky can spot
a pimple on your nose
from outer space

all caught in the world wide web
held in a tiny fishbowl globe
all swimming like green sea turtles
in smaller & smaller
concentric circles

since the horror of mass storage
everyone's a spy working
for the same boss
life became a virtual game
& secrecy a forbidden frequency

the kids don't want to go to bed

i'll pick up my room i'll wash
my hair i promise to be
good for a long long time
any time
but time for bed

they got life to live
& they want to go-go-go
until they can't go no more

right now they say sleep
is a waste of time
& tomorrow a waste of time
because tomorrow never comes

they use any excuse to stay up later
like brushing their teeth for eternity

what the hell are you doing in there?
the kids don't ever want
to go to bed

the kids don't want to get out of bed

i need to finish this dream
i can't get up in the dark
no no don't
turn the lights on
o that hurts my head!

there's no rise & shine anymore
in the once shiny bright
whippersnappers

they want to sleep until noon
because school is a waste of time

those student loans we owe
add up to a lot of dough
even though the sun shines
on easy street
the future looks bleak
& i can't wake them

no no not really
because right now the kids
don't want to get out of bed

kids these days come out of

the womb googling
posting selfies to the universe
& after a little rabbit-hole
research
          they discover vegetables
& animals & tentacles
whipped cream & dark whips
latex & kinky objects
wax play & bondage effects
deals on high heels & leather boots
secret juice & forbidden fruits
uniforms & unicorns
from the church of holy salvation
for our sacred fixations
& god knows what

i imagine god's bored with porn
or wonder if she's watching
the great experiment
from above
          because right now
from where i sit
it's impossible to predict
exactly where this strange trip
of freaky garden delights
might fall

i used to laugh at the kids
          (when they were younger)

they called poetry poke-a-tree
& blurst out dozens of provocative
dada-esque remarks:

tow trucks don't have any feet
skeletons are stuck in our bodies
bats eat butterflies
i can spell yo-yo with my eyes closed
is there a god in the potty?
mind is as slippery as your brain
never dive head-first
into a bowl of ice cream

i relish these times of peril!
in china cats can write
perogies sound like pina coladas
we can't get out the way we come in
better to be cool than handsome
do crabs have testicles?

the earth can't breathe
          until the stars come out

when i was your age i could do it myself
pigs don't eat pigmies
those clouds became dust bunnies
can you come out of the phone?
this is a lightning treble gun
that bald eagle is climbing the wind
what do spiders do for exercise?

there's no such thing as free stealing

frosting is good for the soul
i haven't heard that song since 1903
it's a good day for dancing!
too much TV can outsmart your brain
i want to go shopping for money
life is easy
comedy is really hard

you're in god's world when you dream
in the end nothing's left
but a bug-eyed belch

sometimes the kids surprise me

& take problems of the world
seriously
        as if they could actually
        make a dent of difference

or maybe turn the ship on a dime
before a global climatic
titanic

sometimes they stand at the helm
fearless & full of maxim & proverb

they still believe they have rights
& these laws might help them
create a better place

        how i admire their heroic
        lambs-to-slaughter idealism

i'm both old & young enough
to remember
the 60s
        how our hearts got lighter
        as the games got darker

how we learn to let go

the kids act
as if they don't care

they know we're collapsing
& crashing & relapsing
        yet as long as there's power
        & the internet stays on
they have faith
someone else will repair
& restore order

why don't you fix it dad?
they ask & then i remember
the sunny days my lungs & legs
& confidence
        were so strong
i knew i could do anything
including live forever

i say you think you have time
& mind & prime enough
until it's too late

yet the kids are young
high-strung & wired
        for instant amusement
every unknown tomorrow
an eternity away

the kids seem obsessed with money

they assume cash is king
& abundant bling rules everything

spoon-fed & fuel-injected
from a non-stop laptop podcast
talk-shop pop-throb
hip-hopper teeny bopper

they vow to make the most green
with the least amount of work
no idea no skill no talent
with nothing to risk or invest

they confuse business with money
& money with happiness & poverty
with ignorance & animosity

the kids search for an edge
an angle for leverage on anything

you got something? they ask
they don't care how or what
as long as it rains
        large bills & change

old seahorse remembers when

the world had patience
& most everything moved
at a more humane pace

the poetry of rotary phones
tethered by wire to walls
unequipped with wi-fi screens
or answering machines

we walked places at easy paces
& used the time to muse & unwind

we relished hours of solitude
to reflect on the magnitude of dreams
the analog of paperbound books
or dialogues with friends

interior worlds & words had higher
ceilings & deeper meanings then

screens were a luxury
& everybody watched the radio
as if we could see inside
theatre of the mind

we didn't scurry in such a worry
to go someplace else

we embraced & savored each moment
with the acceptance of presence
not as parents of distress
or adolescence

the honest art of contemplation
guided not divided us

the kids are impulsive

attracted to danger & adventure
shiny flashy sparkly expensive things

they want to feel good feel better
get further out of their disoriented heads

they want to dive into parties & be lost
in a sea of confused beautiful people

they like loud pounding rebellious
raucous & rollus rapper maximus

anything that rattles bones & cages
& rages with their unruly hormones

science reports it takes 25 years
for human brains to fully develop

but kids don't plan they just want
to be kids as long as they can

having kids

i know their job is to give me
white hair & run me
                  faster deeper harder
                  into the ground

get out of the way old seahorse
they say or we'll knock you down

so far
i'm still upright
because i've learned
how to side-step then bend & flow
into the playful phasing of kindness
when to defuse
emotional timebombs
& give myself a timeout
or offer genuine encouragement

how to let go of the last ego clash
over curfew or virtue
the quality of an apology
or how many times
                  you can split a hair
        & see a storm coming
from miles away

the kids are attracted to hyperbole

know the power of amplification
& the magic of imagination

i avoid stepping on sidewalk cracks
& never wear green on thursday

the kids battle hackers & viruses
& 24-hour spies in all their devices

i told you a million times
not to exaggerate i used to say

yet everyday a new exponential
threatens every expectation

everyday modern conveniences
become more inconvenient

everyday the virtual world
consumes a byte more reality

the kids grew up with

endless war & polarized politics
unblind justice & eroding civil rights

i worry the kids might believe
that's the natural balance
of civilization

is mother earth a sentient being?

where does conditioning end
& brainwashing begin?

when is a trillion not enough?

how much more abuse
in the name of god & greed
can our spaceship take?

how long can survival mode last?

when will george orwell
conveniently disappear?

what do you want to be when

                        you grow up?
i watch them squirm
just like i did at their ages
as if we should know so soon
as if anyone could ever really know

so just like me i see them make things up
to satisfy random grown-ups
overly concerned with the future

they discover the words
doctor or lawyer
stop the silly interrogation
               so they can continue
playing video games

intuitively the kids know growing up
is a state of mind & control

there's power in staying young
keeping yourself
from falling into the traps of the system
that job us & rob us & stop us
from growing forever

the powers that be

i tell the kids
the powers that be don't want
you to meditate

they don't want you to stop spending
they don't want you to stop taking drugs
& the new flavored drink
they don't want you to read or think
or stop watching sports or the war
on your screens

they don't want you to stop
playing video games
they don't want you to question
the system or tradition
they don't want you to vote
or toss your remote
they don't want you to live off the grid
or conquer your crutch
they don't want you to make
too much
or too little money

they don't want you to stop trying
they don't want you to try too hard
they don't want you to think for yourself
or worry about the suffering of others
they don't want you to veer
they don't want you to truly care

too many powers that be
don't want you to be
anything more
than clones of each other
in your large enough for more
3-D homes

breaking out

kids these days just want to escape
take a long vacation
                    from the loop of resist
& the blind coffee bean grind
of teenage wasteland

you can tell in their fashion & lingo
their reaction to education
their sweeteners of coconut creamers
their music & attitude
their rebellion against rebellion
or whatever the old seahorses
keep pushing & pulling

watch how they fall from skateboards
& laugh as if the world is one big
slapstick jackhammer

not all their fault because young brains
have growing pains & sometimes
seems everything explodes
around them
                    then someone offers
                    a temporary way out
            & they take a few pills
or drinks or puffs
& make a moody detour or two

hard to know which way to go
in that spiral trial of tailspin
when all you really want for them
is to grow up
& shed their own skin

no power shortage in

the energy of kids
their minds & bodies & spirits
plugged into our larger network
that feeds a greater grid
that fuels a higher purpose
to pulse & drive the matrix
pirouette outlet to go
into perpetual flow

3-21-144-987-6765 deep & deeper

everyone buzzing in worldwide hive
powers to the power to the power
greater than the sum

fibonacci spirals speaking youth
master wonders multiplying themselves
new supernatural existential
consequential essential potential
everything drumming running
humming & loving as one
except
          humans get attracted to chaos
& distraction & our urgent surges merge
with the entropy of energy

those pesky laws of thermodynamics
won't reverse our economics
another case of accidental dissolve
fading flagging withering flowers
& backwards we revolve
          to look again into the sun

the kids don't want to know

about history or dead emperors
or warriors or dates & places & wars
long before they were born

they say it's okay if we don't carry
these useless things in our heads
we have them all in our phones
& tablets at our command
                                    24/7
besides what can we do
about water under the bridge?

            how civilizations collapse
into black hole doughnuts
& hollow circuses
then unwise wars to feed military affairs
or the inequality of poverty
slavery & trillionaire robbery
why there's no intelligence
in the arrogance of racism
the cultural suicide of genocide
the delicate balance of capitalism
science & nature
with the curse of clownish egos
verses wisdom of the universe

our anthem of mantras drones:
we're doomed to repeat doomed
to repeat doomed to repeat...

the older i get the more echo patterns
of tragedy & catastrophe i notice
with clarity how history teachers
fail us by not using the past
as a mirror

i told the kids for years

one of the secrets of success:
stay flexible

you never know when you'll need
to bow this way or that
& in the long run
humbly twisting the better way
is a lot easier than breaking
bracing or bleeding

yet protective effective flexibility
requires daily attention
mentally & physically stretching body
& expanding mind
          in diverse directions

as much about preparation
as prevention
a type of ascension
into special dimension

handy in studio chateau or rodeo
nature neighbor or labor
even boardroom or bedroom

never goes out of style

look at your trash i warn the kids

my oil-driven generation created
more disposable junk than
100 generations before

      mad plastic casket world

know yourself but also know
what you throw away

      scrutinize your ties to waste

everything has to go somewhere
even old seahorse babble
clutters as it vibrates into space

      murmuring to far-flung galaxies

i counsel the kids to reduce mental
physical & spiritual trash

      advise no emotional hoarding

yet the first step:
knowing the difference
between gold & dross

      bare floor needs sweeping

perpetually learning
how to make something
worth keeping
to let go
      let go
          let go

once i was so delusional

       i thought i had parenting
under control

convinced myself domestic order
depended on the little things
like routine & bribery
with modest treats

back when the kids believed
a great reward for good behavior
was an ice cube
            until they visited next door
      & the neighbors gave them
      a srawberry popsicle

upon their return one acted
as if he'd stolen fire
from the gods

the other permanently perplexed
at my culinary incompetence

raising expectations

they complain of suffering
& wonder why life hurts so much
when they're not old enough
to scratch the surface
of ache & pain

they complain of suffering
& wonder if there's safe medication
to take a short vacation

they complain of suffering
& wonder if it ever stops or slows
enough to ease the pressure
so i tell them the suffering
only gets better

the pain the sting the angst
the anxiety the worry the sorry
the vanity of humanity
& bitter misery of personal history
this thorough agony of sorrow
& enduring woe without relief
from the loyalty of grief

yet i conclude with a brief lesson
from a good friend who used to say
joy is your greatest weapon
joy is your greatest weapon
joy is your greatest weapon

the kids don't want to fall in love

they've seen enough at home
parents squabbling about parenting
or money or vacuuming or how
clean is a clean toilet

they've seen enough baby-making
& bloody childbirth on their screens

they've seen enough at the park
all that young spring backseat
button fumbling trees flowering
dogs sticking bees buzzing loop

looks like too much trouble
like someone's gonna get stung

or something too young might break

the kids don't know too much

of anything
yet they think they do

i know less than nothing –bill bissett
& that almost says too much
when it comes to knowledge

wisdom is another matter

to become a reliable sage you must
punch the clock of experience
& tame the tai chi tiger
of effortless effort

but the kids watch too many
summer blockbusters
where some six-packed muscled
superpowered
          caped comic hero
saves the world
in a couple of hours

longer than it takes to let go
empty your mind
& relax into the flow

the kids don't know nietzsche

yet they say what doesn't kill me
makes me cynical

i understand
        there's comfort in sarcasm
        though not a lot of action

we exchange passive aggressive
chuckles
        while rome is burning
        with the rest of the world

how much more sardonic
can you get

        before we don't care
about drinkable water
& breathable air

when i was a kid the big Now thing

was the space-age genius of convenience
original astronaut orange flavor
just add water & stir
or the new improved just add water
& no muss no fuss no stir at all
easy speedy seltzer plus
have yourself a happy fizzies party!

the magic of modern technology
& better living through chemistry
the easy fleeting ecstasy of suddenly
all the rage in the atomic age
every push-button recipe
delicious nutritious miraculous
& mushroom-cloud religious

instant belief instant relief
instant mashed potato instant mayo
instant coffee instant cocoa
instant credit instant payment
instant cake mix instant quick-fix
instant oatmeal instant sex-appeal
instant pleasure instant pudding

TV dinners & hamburger helpers
minute maid & minute rice
pre-washed pre-tossed & pre-sliced
faster sooner quicker swifter
pop tarts & instant pop charts
perma-press & stove top dressing
imitation flavors emotional time-savers
acres of colors of disposable razors

yet today the kids want everything yesterday
brand newer improved & breakthrough
brought to you by wizards in a blizzard
free expedited billing to your home
by AI robot drone with triple the shipping
plus porch pirate insurance

& turbo gizmo video-tracking faster disaster
moneyback guarantee master card
as if credit grows on money trees
as if tomorrow is delivered too late
as if super-extra-instant convenience
ever made a whit of difference

old seahorse says the game is

on the line & we're getting down
to crunch time

      the kids laugh
      & say we're not like you
      we're built different
      we know we're millennial
      we got the world on a string

old seahorse replies your string theory
is too literal to contain quantum

      we can still party in the aquarium
      of quantum they reply

old seahorse says remember
your heart connection
to mother earth

      one of the kids says
      if everyone's connected
      why do i feel so alone?

old seahorse says the planet is melting
yet creation remains wave & vibration
wave & vibing vibration

dive in the ocean
      bathe in the forest
          contemplate sky

everything passes he says
but nothing good ever dies

the growing pains of

a teenage brain will drive you
half-insane up & down the highway
of change on a mission without permission
for something vaporous & dangerous

there's nothing they don't know
or nothing you know better

than their angular post-modern
obtuse cubist self-abuse faceless
stainless tasteless contagious
deep-fried matrix world

driven out of wormhole control
into a mad labyrinth prism

projecting acres of layers & spectrums
of flavors for razorblades of intentions
multiplied by levels of demons
& heavenly devils

a new kind of beast unleashed
in your weevil steeple home

every generation a new insurrection
another mother/father mutation
to become the master of faster power
at their joystick quicksand command

some cynical kids get obsessed with bukowski

he's their champion
their anti-lifestyle coach
& wasted poetic guru
the inspiration for lost weekends
& writing their insides out
in see-through language

but somewhere up there
hank's not moved or amused
he knew he wasn't a hero
to place on a pedestal
& he's horrified by
so many middle-class clones
attempting to emulate
his uncorked cravings
& warped tortured soul

imagine his raw invisible welts
the muse of purple bruises
donated by daddy's razor strap
peer into his cratered face
the adolescent volcanic pox
souvenir depressions squeezed
from a thousand bloody ugly
pus-packed eruptions

he'd be the first to tell the kids
you're trying too hard
he'd say get your own life baby
your own symptoms
your own system & stop betting on
        a dead seahorse
to carry you across
the finish line

i'm an old seahorse now &

all the kids got skinny scrawny gaunt
& wafer-wasted-thin
          their scraggy jagged manes
          thick & riotous
or asymetrical lopped & too close-cropped
their harsh imaginations dull & tame
anti-this anti-that
more attitude than platitude
more herd & nerd & wi-fi slurred

another carbon form of urban speak
& high-tech jargon shrink-rapped
in torn skin-tight threads of black & grey
they recede into the elbows
of shadows
camouflage for uber-lurking

their music without intricate muse
nothing mysterious or too sadly serious
the same unamusing three beats
beating melody beating
harmony bleeding my eardrums
with relentless bang-bang precision

the endless entropy of mechanical grinding
they collide contort & flail
till coat of arms & princess crowns fall off
then grow faux wings or unicorn horns
with platform hooves
                         spry girls prance
on painted pony feet or high-rise
combat boots that rattle
smart-phone libidos & star-dust bones
as they dance on my waiting grave

the loop of innocence lost

the kids want to grow up
before their time

they start shaving peach fuzz
& spending your credit
they want a car
before they earn a driver's license
a professional guitar
before they read music

      they want to start dating
for all the wrong reasons
they throw parties
when i'm out of town

         i mourn innocence lost
& the birth of being eaten alive
by society
     all-consumed by consumerism
the collective cliches of common
teenage obsession

just like that there's no turning back
& no turning your back
on turning back

when i was a kid i used walk to skid row

on sunday mornings to study
the forgotten men at victory square

liquor stores were closed
& their blood craved thinning

a somber sober hungover haze
draped across this wounded

brooding veteran community
alcoholics without alcohol

only dawned on them after 10am
so they pooled their pocket coin

& sponsored an expedition
to a drugstore for aftershave

naïve as the strutting pigeons
pecking at discarded crumbs

i thought the rock-bottom blues
of these faded crusaders

would somehow bring me
closer to the truth

welcome to the age of reduction

old men don't want to complain or feel worthless or
out of step with progress or regress or bag groceries
at payless or greet shoppers at walmart or polish floors
on the corporate nightshift or play endless games of
dominoes in any dark melancholic neighborhood park

they don't want to sit in blurry bars with strangers
drinking shots of nostalgia or live their last few years
surrounded by faded memorabilia & naked dementia

old men don't want to be jaded outdated or isolated
become cynical or radical because everybody else
became too normal they don't want to open junk mail
about life insurance credit cards or cremation services
they don't want to read more obituaries about friends
& lovers or watch TV about old people watching TV

they don't want to constantly search for the right word
or name or place or forget what they had for breakfast
yet still drink in the fresh heady scent of a firstgirlfriend

old men don't want to stay in bed all morning or forget
to shave the left side of their face or where they
parked their car or drive with the parking brake on or
leave a fly undone or lose the keys or lock themselves
out or forget again what they were trying over & over
to remember

old men don't want to think their life had no meaning
or make up tales about how they attained greatness &
had enough brushes with fame to drop names like rain

they don't want to fantasize all the beautiful talented
intelligent wonderful generous women who loved them
& how once upon a time they were greek gods
between the sheets

no old men don't want to get older & slower & broker
& lost in the thick strange of material planes

old men don't want to end up unknown in green rooms
on a morphine drip watching IV bags drip-drop & sweat
holding some kid's hand as they ride off

into the sunset

the kids think i'm a little crazy

they whisper to their friends
      he's into conspiracy theories

they say he believes in ghosts
spaceships from other galaxies
interdimensional beings
forever chemicals
& genetic poison in our food

they speak as though education
stunted their imaginations

i tell them to keep open minds
talk to animals & more importantly
learn how to listen to them

i say don't let the system
interfere with your education

i remind the kids to grow
      in all directions
think with the deepest part
of their hearts
learn to feel with brains

wonder what kind of planes
melt hundreds of steel girders

old seahorse compares

                    the best of his youth
to today's malaise of mediocrity

music art movies & travel
used to be a thousand times better
fifty or more years ago he rails

the kids don't care
they have internet & AI
& they're stars of their own
virtual reality

what's theatre? they say
i am the stage!

but the kids don't know brando
twombly beefheart or wandering
backstreets of old kathmandu
they scoff at fellini duchamp
zappa beckett or the holy vibration
on the steps of borobudur
no patience for tarkovsky
dostoevsky kandinsky gretzky
or a bike-ride across canada

seems everything shifted
                    a million miles sideways
in a few short years
now old seahorse feels wistful
a little betrayed by machines
& screens & virtual dreams

but the kids don't care
they're not into compare
& already onto the next

old seahorse talk

get the hell off my lawn!
you're too young to understand
the history books are wrong
                    i know because
             i was there
if i was younger
i'd turn you over my knee
             turn the music down
             or i'll turn it off!
no you can't have your ball back
i know music when i hear it
& that's noise
        back in my day
        we knew how to have fun
        without money
you got no respect
for yourself
when i was your age
everything was miles better

        the kids roll their eyes
& can't wait to leave
the room

so whadda YOU know about

love? the kids threaten
then add a twist of the knife
you've been divorced two times

i tell them
          you learn more about love
after your heart's been broken
cause that's when it grows the most

you can't just glue & patch
& pump it up like a punctured tire
then roll obliviously happy
up main street again
you need to hurt & bleed
& babble into bottles
or howl at the reflection
of the moon in your tears

take more time than you think
you need to break & ache
mend & meditate
carve out the hooks & barbs
sever the cords of words & bonds
lick your ego wounds
& glide past opaque gloom

no secret equation will give you
an all-clear prediction

eventually you realize
love moves in one direction
love can only expand
& then you'll know love needs
somewhere to go & maybe
someone to receive

when i skipped school

i sauntered to the sign
of the seahorse called hippocampus
ordered fries
          flooded them with malt vinegar
& made it rain black pepper

then walked a block to english bay
where I sat on hard wet sand
hid behind a huge
fugitive log
& zoned out to the dreamy echoes
of seagulls & fog horns
lazily gazed on soft splintered light filtered
through towering cedars
& rolled with the endless ripple
of holy water on sacred shore
my private escape
my break-out from the dulling factory
of oppressive fluorescence
& the clockwork boxes
of 20-minute pods

my eighteen virgin years cried out
for more green less grey
more expansion less sanction
                    more nature less man

except those hot hand-cut chips
always hit the spot

nothing new under the sun

they complain they whine
they want they take they love
they eat they spend they worship
they destroy they rebel

they break each other's hearts
& sometimes they break
their parents' hearts

they take chances & make advances
they blush & rush into romances
they milkshake they headache
they heartache they bellyache
they outbreak they intake
they mime they rhyme
they crash they dash in a flash
they don't have time for time

trial & error & error & trial
sometimes they learn it's tribal
sometimes it's pure survival
sometimes it's undeniably denial
yet sooner or later the kids grow up
then shake their heads

at the next new gang of fresh
& brash who think they're the first
to be cursed with a thirst to do
everything all over again

i used to chase after the kids

but when my oldest started to run
faster than me
                    i fit him into a harness
& that worked until he launched
a sit-down strike in the middle
of a busy mall
                    refused to move
as i pulled on the leash while he pulled
on the heart-strings
of passersby

when i wasn't looking
my youngest soundlessly skulked away
to visit the neighbors with no one home
watched TV as if he owned the place
while i went half-insane
thinking he'd been abducted
by a local pack of hungry coyotes

the first time my 4-year-old saw
a bowling alley he thought
it was a race track
like a fool i chased him past the foul line
fell flat on my back
& stayed in bed for three days

now old enough to leave home
                    defiant dissent fading
they don't want to go
they don't really want to go

when i was a kid my old man used to say

you'd lose you head if it wasn't
                    screwed on
life doesn't get better for the complainers
the biggest losers never try
excuses don't know how to finish
never be satisfied
make time
roll with the punches
you don't know the value of a dollar
the worst feeling in life is when
you beat yourself
if brains were gunpowder you wouldn't
have enough to blow your nose
you can if you think you can
make time
the difference between good & great
is a little extra effort
drive yourself
drive yourself through the finish
work your turns
finish hard
           don't worry about pain
                    pain goes away
go tell your mother she wants you
there's always room for improvement
find your own way home
            make time
make time
drive yourself drive yourself
never be satisfied

every part of the universe is

in flux
          i tell the kids:
          you're no exception

everything fluid & flowing
every moment a wave of teaching
a pivot to something greater

i say turn your spigot to spirit
be a creator not a hater
who knows i echo maybe you'll catch
a thimble of wisdom

they don't realize this yet
but the grave lessons of change
never stop drooling

the great universal teachings
expand & flow
          even when blood is old
& body shrinking

especially
when old & shrinking

even the youngest is in on my act

he says i worry about the kids
these days

one took a teddy bear
to middle school
                full of marijuana

they banned water bottles
at high school
because too many kids
spike their water with booze

the town just hired 20 more cops
& they're putting one
in our school

i don't know what's next he said
but any fool can predict
something bad
                is bound to happen

old seahorse equation

       the older you get
the stranger the world becomes

the hamster wheel & the great seal
the rabbit holes & rabbit paroles
the i ching teaching of moral reef bleaching
the mouse maze into the next phase
the treadmills of the anthills
& the ceaseless nature
of elliptical future

      the more you find yourself
watching & talking to sky

the me in me

gets smaller & quieter
every year

i know exactly what he wants

how he pushes my buttons
tries to fool me
                into thinking
        i'm less important
than someone else

i watch the kids play

see them wrestle
with loops of screaming me me!

intermittenly
their me gets the best of them
in the worst possible way

into the what

we loop & loop into the game
again & again but what does it mean
to repeat the same scene?

we all need new loopholes
to move beyond the counterview
if we only knew
the best way out is through

everybody wants to know exactly
where to go but isn't what
more important than where?

is there any what worth making?
is there any what worth saving?

every thought a what
every what a wave
every wave an equation
of infinite quantum
that vibrates out of mind

because anyone can think
a thousand thoughts before lunch
but what will you achieve or find?
what will you leave behind?

make time to empty

sometimes the kids need to talk
& the parents just need to listen

no judgement no advice
no problem no solution no fight
no politics in the tricks tonight

just make room to make room
let deeper thoughts into the dome

remove those alarm-clock blocks
clear those spam-fueled logjams
flush that blackout doubt

move your blah-blah to the trash
empty your ashtray cache

delete those files of angry loops
& everyone moves lucidly fluently
beautifully forward & onward

no crucifix in the mix tonight
nothing to predict or fix tonight

to love & forgive with permission
sometimes the kids need to talk
& the parents just need to listen

rebellion against rebellion

I love when the kids show me
extra moxie
                          when they get
all pumped up on themselves
& want to take on
the world

please please do it do it I say
upset the tree of knowledge apple cart
& make all this better
          than global materialism

god knows we need to transform
transcend & evolve primal mind

then they give me that *wha?* blank look
like i just ruined their private
revolution
                    because how revolting
                    could their revolt be
with a crazy old seahorse
cheering them on

kids love new stuff

especially solar-powered toys
battery gadgets with whim-whams
& widgets with doo-dads
watches & glasses & cameras & screens
in all the colors & combinations
of nature & imagination
for music & communication
& connection with apps
for maps & cheats for seats
& self-help with yelp or an injection
of self-affection
jesus
there's even an app
for resurrection
a fresh generation of new units
for the same market
once every few months
cause they know the kids are addicted
to the newest fangled
        fashion-accessory heroin
every day digging & picking
& feeding
our modern burdens
from the hothouse garden
of electronic eden

one of the kids bought some stock &

asks my opinion of his venture savvy
yet sadly i offer little insight

stocks are a millionaire's game
watching numbers go up & down
while the working man bales hay
for the rich man's livestock

i tell him buy low & sell high
but he's already bought high

one day he's up & excited
the next he's down & depressed
& i say that's what you invited
because numbers have no soul

he threatens to cash out but then
he'll lose $2 & eighty-nine cents

he acts disgusted with how much
he watches that app & i'm not proud
to say they feed on a captive flock
to chase the lost sheep crowd

spending time wisely i say
is the most valuable currency

growing in

                    any fool can tell
the kids are growing up
a little overnight

then they make their way each day
through that brand new hole
they punch
in the universe

            i applaud brava! bravo!
& egg them on
except
            i know growing up
            is less about going out
than making friends
with yourself

northwest kids don't mind

the perpetual drizzle of winter rain
they grow up with wet hair
dry humor green vision
& damp shoulders

they bathe in grey days for weeks
seek cedar forest shelter
& wrap themselves
in blankets of season-change fog

they speak fluent raven
know where the mushrooms spawn
intuitively sense when orca pods
are coming to town

they make friends with coyote
gather plump berries on the path
predict weather in the moss
laugh at the loop of hurry

forest kids understand the power
of the land before white men arrived
with their sharp-tooth religion
& crucified original trees

yet the kids grow optimystic
& shamanistic
they see ancestors in the mist
know protesters in their midst

they wait for new patches of blue
under canopy of dancing branches
they anticipate warmer winds
& watch magic expand

the victory of seahorse defeat

when my oldest was five
he beat me at chess
pinned my king in a corner
within six moves

i know what you're thinking
i wouldn't or couldn't let him win
against every fiber of my competitive
brainwashing

yet he served me more than
a large slice of humble pie
my ego both devasted
& triumphant

how badly do you want it?

so much of life becomes
a matter of will

the everyday courage to fail
the fortitude to believe in yourself
the backbone to dismiss
self-doubt
                              the inner calm
                    to quiet outer chaos

but the kids think greatness is easy
renown comes natural & talent
a silver spoon
inherited from thin air

they wish for a magic formula
to change their genes
a bottle of fame
or a case of success
to gently land in their laps
to please their lips
& expand their money clips

i never let them forget
90% of life is merely showing up
the other unshaped half
what you create

kids watch star wars but

they don't trust crop circles
missing links or close encounters
of any kind

they don't believe aliens
will save us from ourselves
teach us teleportation
or show us the way through
wormholes to new dimensions
& higher vibrations

the kids aren't waiting
for a sudden intervention
from another solar system

they say human problems
need human solutions

& praying for a cosmic miracle
is a little like expecting the parents
to finish this school work
& clean up our rooms

the good news about illusion

i tell the kids happiness is
all in your mind
it doesn't depend on anyone
or anything
                  except you

it's love & fear & pain & woe &
joy & sorrow & pleasure
& laughter & crying &
waiting &
                  aging & losing & winning
& wonder & winter & summer &
sickness & wealth & fame
& health & poverty &
family & friends
                  & facts & fiction
& beauty & decrepitude

ahhhhh the truth & beauty
of decrepitude
                  how the mind plays
         with assorted shades
& depth of light

the kids love japanese films

japanese manga & japanese food
yet they struggle with zen

how a whack on the back
might jolt one from monkey mind
into wakefulness
how all music is created
by the silence   between   notes
how sitting still
can become great action

        how everything is nothing
& nothing is everything

they don't get it   yet

but the kids feel compassion for godzilla
they empathize with his frustration
& marvel at his destructive
prowess
a genius at the art of obliteration
so rebirth can emerge

                & at the end of the day
        or beginning of an age
sometimes that's
exactly what's needed

occasionally the kids find

a glitch in the matrix
usually a misguided loop program
that can't corkscrew out of itself

& they get stuck repeating
the same mistake
over & over

they become hypnotized
following the trails of orbits
round & round

a glowing axis of pixels
until too many synapses climax
& collapse

then freeze-frame in sprockets
repeat click repeat click
burn yesteryear's film

some kids weary
of the simulated holographic
predictable digital world

sometimes even the old seahorse
needs to be reminded
the improbability of finish

or the magnitude of infinity
& that just might be
our greatest responsibility

bitter sweet blood song

bloodlines run deep & fast
everything humbles & blunders on
as somehow few threads last

this chosen unbroken unspoken
flood of blood between mothers & fathers
to sons & daughters cannot be undone
so we pass it on & on
          rejoice in sweet embrace

we all exist on this
booming human spectrum
of imperfection
                with trickles of bitter
          whipped into the mix
to balance the talents
of ego & bliss

how we come together & fall apart
circle back to the pumping flow
& beat of the heart

since the beginning of giving
          from the end
to the start
may our blood songs run deep
to the beat of our hearts

advice from seahorse the elder

long ago my father used to
fluctuate between
           quit while you're behind
& *quitters never win*

expressions of contradiction i thought
until i realized context was everything

the former used when arguing with him
& the latter when discouraged
about personal endeavor

experience taught me he was so competitive
no one could win

& if i ever complained about age
rules fairness or size
              he hit me with his closer:
every punker has a good excuse

when I was a kid my mother used to say

you made your bed now lie in it
you've cooked your goose
wait till your father gets home

no one is mature at sixteen
don't traipse dirt all over the house
no playing ball inside

wash your hands before dinner
this kitchen isn't a restaurant
because your father likes liver

life isn't fair
come out when your room is clean
wait till your father gets home

he'll get his comeupance
she's not dealing with a full deck
we all do things we don't want to

my job is to worry
I'm your mother not your friend
you don't smell like a library

brush your teeth & go to bed
because i said so
wait till your father gets home

dear kids

help me see myself at your age
or any age
as long as i see myself
as i am & not
as i think i must be
or believe to be
or want to be
or pretend to be
someone i cannot live up to
wearing coats of exaggerated reputation
phony accomplishments
& non-essential credentials
excuses on steroids
the molecule-thin veneer
of pie-in-the-sky piousness
laced & debased
with self-serving veins
of faux generosity

let me never cast the first stone
or any stone at all

i remember my mother
explaining
> *we're not hypocrites*
> *we just want you*
> *to be better than us*

years ago
(in galaxies far far away)

the kids build their vocabularies
from oral tradition
what they thought they heard
from parents
                    peers & TV

tow trucks became toad trucks
vitamins became vitamints
earthquake became earthshake
milkshake became milk shape
jacuzzi became gucci
chairman mao became sherman mao
sun screen became sun scream
saxophone became axe-a-phone
oatmeal became eatmeal
poetry became poke-a-tree
kleenex became need-ex
& wake up became ache up

i miss that heady steady stream
of happy word accidents
how syrup converted
to sir bop

when milky way translated
to the milky wave

the chemistry of memory

      what is a memory made of?

not experiences turned into neurons
filed away in the belly of the seahorse
but really
      what kind of substance
      are we molding & shaping?

has anyone ever seen a memory?
indisputable visual reality
not reasonable facsimiles or imaginary
recollections based on a true story
from twice removed personal
interpretation

      seems the hippocampus
      is as nebulous as feckless

are memories chemical
electrical or both?
wired to receive patterns of synapses
but why do recollections fade
& why do synapses lapse?

do memories even happen
or are they another trick of the light?
are they stored in the brain
or do we carry them in the cloud
of our hearts?

science reports memories are
a fluid solution made of trace metals
distributed within the matrix
firing on circuits

embedded in neurons
through which gasses diffuse
& fuse with bonding geometrics
made of glutamate

damn
are memories not gluten-free?
perhaps memories are newton free?
who knows if glutamate has an expiry date?
& can it help you find your soulmate?

       or is glutamate that salty stuff
       they put in your chinese food?

surely the mundane sacrifice
of greasy fried rice or gooey egg foo yung
is not the substance that evokes
& retells the best or worst moments
of our lives
       those personal historic times
       that bind & connect us
& make us who we think we are
or have been

or even remember
who we still could become

the kids would've liked my father if

they knew him
          before he lost his mind
& i wonder if the kids will know me
before i lose mine

or will they only remember
the power plays & time-outs
& enraged voices

i ponder if they've forgotten
those first trying nights
i ferberized them
& they cried themselves to sleep

in another room their mother
closed the door & silently wept
couldn't bear to hear them

the ground we walk on
held together by the ghosts
of vanished ancestors
we never fully knew

i tell the kids to push the work

don't let the work
push you
                then they sumo wrestle
        until one of them falls

i remember the day my grandfather
told me to make your hobby
your job

i thought he was crazy

until i saw him playing handyman
carpenter gardener electrician & plumber
in his retirement community

        doing odd jobs for a sandwich
& ice-cold beer

too much of anything

                                    will kill you
i tell the kids long before
they understand natural selection
or middle way

we're all wired to want more
with a need to explore
& expand
                                    no one can walk
            without first learning to fall

i watch the kids use trial & error
to weigh risk & reward
                                    in search of
            the sweet spot between
balance
& impermanence

some people think old age is

10 years older than them
but the kids never let me forget
i'm just an old seahorse

yet i never let them forget
they should live long enough
to be so lucky
because age is just a number
& numbers are abstracts
bloodless
            relative
                        approximations

you can't compare them
to experience nor experience
with wisdom or wisdom with riches
or riches with hunger
& hunger with judgement

perhaps i should offer some pithy
profound advice here
but that's not my purpose
or point
                        for in the end
            if there is an end
you must ask
& answer
your own questions

the news is getting darker

& so is the entertainment
dystopia the hottest movie genre

      i wonder what effect
dismal projections
might have on the kids

in my day we had great invasions
from outer space & monsters
from lost lagoons
but today every end of the world trial
          an amusement park
     of grim cycle
& downward spiral

will the kids grow-up expecting
the aftermath of death
& disaster
         or will we teach them
the sinkhole of control is never-ending
& nature is enormously smarter
more clever & resilient
than man

so whaddaya know about love
(revisited)

the kids don't know it yet but
real love moves you outside yourself

sparks effortless awareness
flows into others & surrounds your field
in completeness & holy emptiness

real love is the furthest thing from
material rings & physical strings

yet its sacred vibration teaches
the art of gift from the spirit place
of the open heart

      real love never gets old
& expands as it grows

although often hard to see
through the layers of fog & stern
your parents intuitively knew this

from the minute you were born
from the instant you were born

that moment when your kid

picks up a lion's mane jellyfish
& the pain so great
he can't catch his breath
& you think both your hearts
might stop

that moment when you see
a neighbor kid throw a rock
       & you hear it
hit your kid with a thud
on the head

that moment when your kid
goes completely limp in your arms
& you're not sure if
           it's already too late
     to go to hospital

that moment when your kid
pokes a hornet's nest & they madly
attack him
even under his shirt
& you must think fast

that moment when a 600-pound
teeter-totter log falls off its fulcrum
& instead of jumping away
your kid holds on

that moment when your kid
calls you from jail & apologizes
for not listening to
your advice

that moment when your kid
gives you a hug & says
i love you dad
i love you

kids are the god particles we seek

they contain the best & worst of us
retain our remedies & memories
& twist our characters
into scores of combinations
we never knew existed

the kids evolve & revolve
around us pushing us past points
while bringing us nearer
they reflect our hopes & fears
in both large & small mirrors

listen to oceans of pulsing blood
the transmission from fission to fusion:
we are the human gods
making heartbraking & forsaking
the particles we seek

we're a carnival of formulas blended
& suspended in mortal portals
an arsenal of articles curled
& swirled into the mutant soup
of ancestors lost & found

we are the gods making the gods
exchanging & changing the next gods
who carry the query
discover the subsequent lover
raise praise & sometimes bury

              the particles we seek
          the particles we teach
the particles we critique

these nostalgia blues

they say everything gets better
in 20 years after the tears have dried
& the pain subsides
                    if it ever does
                    if it ever does

i curse & glorify the past
feel too much too deep too fast
nothing that was will ever last
the good old days feel like a maze
& i'm lost in the age of remembering

i recall wrigley field without lights
5-cent candy bars
19-cent a gallon gasoline
wars fought for worthwhile reasons
when compromise was strength
& policemen could be your friend
i remember black & white TV
with a joyful choice of three channels
15-cent hamburgers
two newspapers a day
morning milk delivered to your door
before computers & spying
on your neighbors
people only took drugs when they were sick
& drug stores didn't sell booze
aisles of junk food
or christmas tinsel in october
i remember the ed sullivan show every sunday
queen for a day with applause meter
to tell the truth
ted mack's amateur hour
when contestants could still get the hook

i can't lose these nostalgia blues

i remember the days before remote control
& power windows & keyless keys
when smoking was so cool they named
a cigarette after it
family dinners & story time
& jiffy pop in the fireplace
when JFK RFK & MLK were gunned down
the day marilyn died & the first man
walked on the moon
i remember service with a smile
when the customer was always right
we all said please & thank you & opened doors
for each other
i can't lose these nostalgia blues

i curse & glorify the past
feel too much too deep too fast
nothing that was will ever last
the good old days feel like a maze
& i'm lost in the age of remembering

i recall when a shot came from a bottle
not a gun & crackerjack toys
were made of metal
we dressed up to ride airplanes
or watch hockey games
sports stars earned five figures
no one ever heard of a billionaire
my mother hated elvis
my father loved pickled beets
my older brother was into UFOs
my younger brother kept on a leash
tied to a tree
& no one called the police

recycling was called the junk business
we only bought antiques
when we couldn't afford something new
suburbia wasn't a dirty word
baked goods weren't kept in the freezer
tarzan was my superhero
ripped wasn't a lifestyle or fashion statement
& dessert always came with every meal
i can't lose these nostalgia blues

i remember when all of us were proud
of our military & old people thought
rock n roll a passing fad
the beatles a flash in the pan
the lawn was mowed every sunday
& marijuana the gateway to heroin
i remember when jimi janis & jim morrison
mama cass & elvis & sinatra died
when andy & beatle john were shot
when duchamp beckett picasso
dali fellini hitchcock & brando died
i remember when leave it to beaver
made us a believer in the american dream
when doctors were gods
a pay-phone call cost a dime
everyone drank tap water
& air quality didn't need warnings
i remember when they were called sneakers
a large cartful of groceries cost 20 dollars
& only the bank could break
a hundred-dollar bill
i can't lose these nostalgia blues

i curse & glorify the past
feel too much too deep too fast
nothing that was will ever last

the good old days feel like a maze
& i'm lost in the age of remembering

i recall a time before seat belts
& air bags & plastic bags & plastic surgery
& plastic razors & plastic pollution
before everything became disposable
including people
i remember when good times were great
movies cost a quarter with at least
one cartoon per feature
baseball cards were 5-cents a pack
& a chance to pull mantle or mays
when kids climbed trees
built forts & made friends face-to-face
our parents always kicked us outside
on summer days & told us
to come home before dinner
when no one had a watch
i remember when cowboys were kings
& we couldn't wait for tomorrow
because everything was better in the future
no sickness no war no crime no poverty
no recession no deep depression of any kind
when we still believed in better living
through chemistry
ford still had a better idea
& coca-cola taught the world to sing
i can't lose these nostalgia blues

i remember when animal farm
was still a kid's book
& 1984 was so far in the future
it could never happen to us
when i thought 30 was over-the-hill
& 16 mature

i remember the late 60s & we all knew
the revolution arrived
but then suddenly the system dangled
their golden carrots & all the good ideas
got swallowed up by corporate armies
in a race to the bottom
for the bottom line

i remember a time before leaf blowers
electric lawn mowers
fake wood floors & dollar stores
because then they were all called 5 & dimes
when a dime was worth a dollar
& dollar an hour was a living wage
i can't lose these nostalgia blues

i curse & glorify the past
feel too much too deep too fast
nothing that was will ever last
the good old days feel like a maze
& i'm lost in the age of remembering

i recall when penmanship
was a major subject at grammar school
cars didn't drive themselves
& little kids believed santa's elves
made all the toys
when old people complained
about the inconvenience of on-line
banking-shopping-dating & email
i remember when postmen were heroes
delivering plastic treasures
from popsicle-wrapper coupon catalogs
& cereal box-tops
before computers cougars hooters & spam
when comic book mail orders

sold us sea monkeys & x-ray specs
& bavarian cuckco-clock barometers
made in japan
before power-tools & powerball & solar power
& powerpoint & girl power
before legos we built with wood blocks
popsicle sticks & tinker toys
i can't lose these nostalgia blues

i remember when failure was not an option
winning was the only thing
                    & nice guys finished last
i remember when health care
didn't break your bank
when apple pie was served with cheese
& the average guy on an average wage
could afford a house in the burbs
because one average wage per family
was enough to keep up
& moving upward
when a new car cost less than five grand
when obsolescence wasn't the first plan
when the world was still a big place
before anyone saw the first picture of earth
from outer space

they say everything gets better
in 20 years after the tears have dried
& the pain subsides
                    if it ever does
                    if it ever does

i curse & glorify the past
feel too much too deep too fast
nothing that was will ever last
the good old days feel like a maze
& i'm lost in the age of remembering

this is the age of accelerated change

3-D printers & virtual reality
quantum computers
                & artificial intelligence
that runs circles around
our tribal minds

but the kids don't seem worried
they chuckle & choose more screen time
their wavy vibrating universe
a robotic dance
for a giant video game

seems only geezers muse nostalgic
for the personal music of cursive
making meals from scratch
holding hands with an analog lover
& walking between forest trees

now science fiction is science fact
& present evidence is piling up
used to be only elders knew
how far is too far past the point
of no return

the kids don't know who they are

they're still searching for role models
& receiving instant icons

everything from cartoons to sorcerers
from superheroes & wizards
to superstars
            from rock gods to fallen angels
shallow sinners to urban saints
affluent influencers
& the ever-popular recycled myth

the progression of imperfection
from pedestal to death

                  i try to guide them
            through the mire of hype
the minefields of blind faith
& the pitfalls of worship

warn them how the faster stars rise
the further they fall
                        they think
because i reject the obvious
the current & common
i want them to be like me
                but i pray someday
        they'll become
themselves

today is easter morning &

i want to get out of bed
& hop around town
collect eggs for my basket
lined with plastic grass
from china but
                    instead I spread out
& laze in bed with poetry books
scratch pads of blank paper
& the quietude
of sunday
                    all my neighbors hungover
            or bored in church or both
thank god the lawn mowers
& leaf blowers are resting
even jesus is just lounging around
ready for liftoff
                    the energy of the kids
                    seems muted today
            busy wolfing
chocolate egg omelets
with sweet & sour hot sauce
butter spread jam-laden toast
& little yellow pan-fried
marshmallow birds

            alone but never alone
i roll away my own stone
i roll away my own stone

some old seahorse refrain

things ain't what they used to be
things ain't what they used to be
things ain't what they used to be
but this old seahorse sez
          WTF how could they be?

life is learning how to let go
& grow into the next

meanwhile the kids embrace routine
as if waffle wednesday
is the third commandment

they seem surprised when computer
tablet phone or old dog dies
but loss & grief
always part of the game
often the most essential byte

all you've become & learned
leads up to the transmission
of your final transition

how you accept change & gravity
with grace & dignity
your personal skeleton key
that opens the great door
to the other side

psychic seahorse muses

does memory play tricks on me?
soften the blows & blur the lines
obscure the clouds & distort the deed
exploit experience & fuzzy the focus
via hippocampus hocus-pocus

does truth get twisted convicted
tilted & bent out of seahorse shape?
do we only imagine our own symmetry?
is function fate & form a body
of shape-shifting synchrony?

are perpetual expectations
always approximations
& abstractions that can never be?
nothing stops changing or aging
nothing bluffing about always becoming

especially in this digital simulation
ones & zeroes get caught up in the chaos
get lost in the shuffle get misplaced
by the haste of a quick cut & paste
in the great kerfuffle of retrieval

does data have a shelf-life?
we can't count on numbers forever
even the meaning of symbols evolve
i remember when infinity
was so much bigger

infinity plus one & that great spreading
shade tree in the garden gnome yard
of my second childhood home
once a budless three-branch twig
in the vast mud of creation

yes yes we breathe-in every tense
all thoughts actions & reveries
we collect & mix-in raves of waves
of partial equation then exhale
the best memories for restoration

did any of my life ever happen?
do we merely dream the dreamer
for another & does it really matter?
as long as we share the same air
with 10,000 generations

some kids think this physical world is

a simulation
god writes the code
& we're all players in the game

first life second life third life
school life play life work life home life
how many truman show alter-egos
do you need?

many life features predetermined
yet selection of options mean
nothing fully certain

       where you live
       who you decide to talk to
       your friends & family
       what you eat inhale & drink
       who you choose to be

parts of the code you edit & rewrite
free will comes with a price
as much rope as you can handle
verdicts you make
or judgements made for you

       choice is a kind of divine
     intervention

destiny resides in your imagination
how you manifest each moment
or passively
let the game play you

he calls every evening

i ask how his day went
& hope (deep breath) for the best

      he says we mopped up vomit
      from a detoxing addict
      or
      we did a deep clean
      of the showers
      or
      i made a no-cook burrito
      out of ramen & rice & dried
      jalapeno & cheese
      & beans

i'll make one for you when i get out
then asks can you read me a poem?

i sigh & read from this collection
scenes from his childhood
when life was in soft
glow focus
            yet in the hard frozen
        moment of past & present
these poems always seem
to point gently
toward our future
                suddenly
a recorded voice interrupts
you have one minute remaining

you can't trust it he says
sometimes it's only 20 seconds
call you tomorrow
love you dad goodbye

karma & luck

everybody needs a little luck
the great producer told me
practice kitchen karma
& clean up after yourself
said the humble poet
my father liked to remind me
you make your own luck

so too with karma
a continuous cosmic balance
of deposit & withdrawal
deposit & withdrawal

but at this moment
the kids don't believe in karma
they want everything now
they think punishment is a crime
& karma takes too long
for the selfish & unkind

the world is a school i say
karma is but one heavy thread
that holds us together
        luck is unpredictable
but always possible
depends on heart intuition timing
action deeds clash attraction
& choices you make

sometimes i give them a lesson
from my music collection

a john lennon song comes on
& we all gleefully sing
instant karma's gonna get you!

my old man used to say

the world isn't waiting just for you
she doesn't care what you're making
she doesn't owe you a living
she doesn't want to know your troubles
she won't stop to pick you up
dust you off dress your wounds
or drive you to your door

the world keeps turning in spite of you
the world will never love you like i do

she's made a billion dollars
before you even opened your eyes
a million more before you touch the floor
no surprise someone's hustling
another fortune before you flushed
you'll never arrive by shuffling or bungling
somewhere the capitol is always dublin

the world keeps turning in spite of you
the world will never love you like i do

is everyone just getting further behind?
is life a game of never catching up?
no chance of ever matching up
this damn country ain't a country club
so don't get stuck in a stale doughnut rut
because right or wrong i'll stay
long enough to write a better song

the world keeps turning in spite of you
the world will never love you like i do

i could tell you 100 stories about

how i fell far short of my own
impatient expectations
but that kind of reflection
perpetuates imperfection
marks a target on your sweater
like a bloody scarlet letter
instead i pray everyday
to the minor god in my mirror
i wish i were a better father
i wish i were a better father

raised by an iron fist
the effects of the great depression
& repression etched on his face
as he told me so bluntly i felt
a little ugly when my father said
you're too old to kiss me goodnight
& tonight i wonder if he ever said
to himself or another
i wish i were a better father
i wish i were a better father

i witnessed sudden surprise
& horror on my own kids' faces
as i whacked them for defiance
& vowed never again violence
because i knew right then
shame grabbed me by the collar
& said repeat after me
i wish i were a better father
i wish i were a better father

some days all my shorcomings
return to taunt & haunt me
into becoming a better human
a better student a better solution
a better friend a better godsend
a better artist a better author
a better lover a better brother
a better cook a better cleaner
a better healer a better speaker
a better buddha a better santa
even a better ordinary me

most days i stutter & suffer
as my relentless mantra gets stronger
& stronger until there's nothing
in the core of nevermore
this plea won't bother
i wish i were a better father
i wish i were a better father

I've seen the old seahorse

with a broken-down memory
how easily he struggles & stumbles
          no input no output
filing system scorched & warped

order of chaos cannot be restored
the tiny librarians left his brain trust

forever erasing recent present
always living in the now
a reocurring nightmare loop
of never-knowing or remembering

the world stops making fate yet
creates more space & less time

you even forget who you are
& where you live
every moment a quandary
your hippocampus is deep fried

you've lost your marbles & mittens
& misplaced your taste for survival

the kids are a test

they challenge expectations
& dash my best dreams for them
in a thousand detached
          tangents & fragments

i pick them up & examine
every shard of reflective surface

see myself in each thought or piece

contemplate my projections
my bloodline my disappointments
my illusions my divine
          my muses my questions
my insecure dimensions

i clean up the mess
& recalibrate my hopes
with less expectation
                    more attention
          more perception

much less perfection

when i was the sisyphus of seahorses

the gods gave me rip tides
heart-breaking waves
& 100s of offspring to carry

with no end to worry
& no time for sorry

everyday a new crisis
everyday a greater mistake
wrapped in layers of labors

millions more memories
to push against the present

the traumas of dramas
etched in my hippocampus
sorrows we cannot forget

the invisible boulders of life
we carry for the next herd

postscript

you trusted us & we thought
we knew better

        we followed the rules
        sang the anthems marched in line
        ate the pesticides before us
        drank the fluoride
        the plastic the chlorine
        & heavy metals
        coming out of our faucets

my mother's mantra
your father & i did the best we could
& i'm sure that's true

nonetheless every generation
gets hoodwinked by something:
business politics chemistry
the psych of new psychology
technology & heaven help us
military intelligence

we operated under the best
brainwashing of the times

ultimately we all need to make
retractions & corrections
become humble & apologize
to the kids for our deceptions
projections & misconceptions

Stephen Roxborough
is the middle of three children.

What are the odds of his older brother growing up to be the world's foremost oddsmaker and his younger brother a Catholic Mormon?

He was raised by his Canadian father, business executive, and age group swim coach, and his American mother who made whipped wax candles, fabric angels, award-winning quilts, and 14 different kinds of Christmas cookies. They were married 64 years.

His Canadian grandfather graduated as far as grade 8, yet became Chairman of the Toronto Board of Education. His American grandfather was an inventor for Bell Telephone, and secretly wanted to become a minister.

The author raised two boys from diapers to high school. He knows there's no retirement from parenting, and works at writing, photography, and being a better father.

Also by Stephen Roxborough

this wonderful perpetual beautiful (2011)

open heart sutra surgery (2013)

ego to earthschool (2017)

the DNA of NHL (2017)

i feel your doughnut pain (2020)

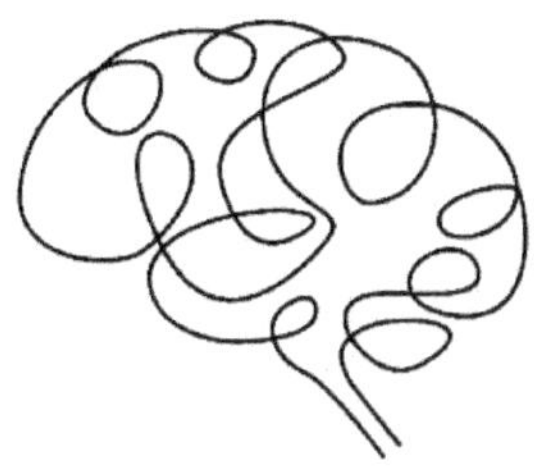